I'm Going to the UK to see the Queen!

Geography for 3rd Grade

Children's Explore the World Books

Queen Elizabeth II has been queen of the United Kingdom of Great Britain as well as Northern Ireland since February 6, 1952. She surpassed Victoria in 2015 as the longest-reigning monarch during British history. In this book, we will explore her life, family and accomplishments.

Her Early Years

Born on April 21, 1926 in London, England, Elizabeth was the firstborn daughter of Albert, the duke of York, along with Lady Elizabeth Bowes-Lyon, his wife. Elizabeth did not have much hope of inheriting the throne, being the child of King George V's younger son.

LONDON, ENGLAND

KING GEORGE VI OF ENGLAND

On December 11, 1936, her uncle, Edward VII (who later became the duke of Windsor), stepped down in favor of her father on December 11, 1936, and her father then was crowned King George VI, and the princess then became his probable heir.

Her mother supervised her education, and entrusted her two daughters to Marion Crawford, a governess. C.H.K. Marten grounded her in history, followed by the Eton College provost.

ETON COLLEGE

PRINCESS MARGARET

The princess also was instructed in languages and music by visiting teachers. Along with Princess Margaret Rose, her sister, they spent a lot of their life during World War II safely apart from the blitz of London; living apart from both of their parents, mostly staying in Scotland at the Balmoral Castle, as well as staying at the Windsor Castle, the Royal Lodge, and Windsor.

Princess Elizabeth accompanied the king and queen on a trip to South Africa early in 1947. After she returned, an announcement was made of her betrothal to a distant cousin, Lieutenant Philip Mountbatten of the Royal Navy and formerly Prince Philip of Denmark and Greece. The marriage occurred on November 20, 1947 in Westminster Abbey.

QUEEN ELIZABETH WITH PRINCE PHILIP

PRINCE CHARLES

The night before her wedding, her father, who was the king, bestowed upon Philip the titles of Baron Greenwich, earl of Merioneth, and duke of Edinburgh. They moved into the Clarence House, located in London. Prince Charles, was their first child, born at Buckingham Palace on November 14, 1948.

Taking over the Throne

As a young lady at the beginning of her reign in the 1950s, she was seen as a "fairytale Queen". It was now a time of hope, following the trauma of WWII, and an era of achievement and progress heralding this as a "new Elizabethan age". In 1957, the accusation by Lord Altrincham that her speeches were similar to those of a "priggish schoolgirl" was one of very few criticisms.

During the latter part of the 1960s, attempts were made portraying a modernistic image in a television documentary titled **Royal Family** and in televising the investiture of Prince Charles as the Prince of Wales. She could be seen wearing overcoats that typically were solid in color along with decorative hats, which allowed her to be easily seen when in a crowd.

King George VI's health took a serious turn during the summer of 1951, and Princess Elizabeth would represent him at various state occasions, including the Trooping the Colour. She and her husband, on October 7, went on a very successful tour of Washington, D.C. and Canada.

WASHINGTON, D.C.

KING GEORGE VI

After spending Christmas at home in England, they went on a tour of New Zealand and Australia in January of 1952, however, along the way, while they were in Kenya, they received news of the death of the king on February 6, 1952.

Now queen, Elizabeth immediately returned to England. She spent the next three months, mourning her father, in comparative seclusion. By the summer, she moved to Buckingham Palace, undertaking routine duties of the sovereign and proceeded, on November 4, with her first state opening of Parliament. Her coronation took place on June 2, 1953 at Westminster Abbey.

BUCKINGHAM PALACE IN LONDON

QUEEN ELIZABETH II IN NEW ZEALAND

The queen and duke took an around-the-world, six-month, tour of the Commonwealth starting in November of 1953. This trip included the first visit to New Zealand and Australia by reigning Britain Monarchy. After visits to several European nations in 1957, they visited the United States and Canada.

She proceeded to make the first tour by royal British of the subcontinent of India in 50 years during 1961.

Additionally, in 1968, she became the first reigning Britain monarchy to visit South America, as well as the countries of the Persian Gulf in 1979.

QUEEN ELIZABETH II IN CANADA

In 1977, during her "Silver Jubilee", she presided over a London Banquet that was attended by leaders of the 36 Commonwealth members; she traveled all around Northern Ireland and Britain; including travelling overseas in the Caribbean, Australia and the South Pacific, as well as Canada.

Once Queen Elizabeth became Queen, Prince Charles was now the heir apparent; and on July 26, 1958 he was named as prince of Wales and on July 1, 1969, became so invested.

PRINCE ANDREW, THE DUKE OF YORK

Her other children were Princess Anne, born on August 15, 1950 (Anne Elizabeth Alice Louise); Prince Andrew, born on February 19, 1960 (Andrew Albert Christian Edward, who was named in 1986 as the Duke of York; and Prince Edward, born on March 10, 1964 (Edward Anthony Richard Louis).

All of her children bear the surname "of Windsor"; however, Elizabeth decided in 1960 to create the name Mountbatten-Windsor for additional descendants that were not titled princess or prince and royal highness. On November 15, 1977, Elizabeth's first grandchild was born (Princess Anne's son).

QUEEN ELIZABETH AND PRINCE PHILIP'S GRANDCHILDREN

The Modern Monarchy

Queen Elizabeth became more and more aware of the modern-day role of the monarchy. One such example is allowing, in 1970, televising the domestic life of the royal family as well as condoning the dissolution of her sister's marriage. However, in the 90s, they would face many challenges.

In 1992, she saw the separation of Prince Charles and his wife, Diana, the Princess of Wales as well as the separation of Prince Andrew and his wife, Sarah, the Duchess of York. Furthermore, Anne was divorced, and the royal residence of the Windsor Castle was gutted by fire.

PRINCE CHARLES AND PRINCESS DIANA

The country was now struggling with a recession, resentment mounted over the lifestyle of the royals, and while personally exempt, in 1992, the Queen agreed to pay income taxes on her private income.

The separation of Charles and Diana (who was tremendously popular), along with divorce in 1996 eroded support of the royals, which sometimes was viewed as unfeeling and antiquated. After the 1997 death of Diana, the criticism was intensified, particularly after the queen at first would not allow the flying of the national flag at half-staff over the Palace.

PRiNCESS DiANA

Following her earlier attempts to modernize the monarchy, she subsequently tried to appear less-traditional and less-stuffy, which attempts were received with mixed success.

Elizabeth would celebrate fifty years on the throne in 2002. Events would be held throughout the Commonwealth as a part of her "Golden Jubilee", including many days of festivities occurring in London. However, with the death of her sister and mother in the early part of the year, the celebrations were diminished to some extent.

QUEEN ELIZABETH'S MOTHER

PRINCE WILLIAM AND PRINCESS CATHERINE

The royal family's standing with the public began to rebound, and Charles's marriage to Camilla Parker Bowles in 2005 found a lot of support. Elizabeth led the royal family in April of 2001, with the celebration of the wedding of the oldest son of Charles and Diana, Prince William of Wales, to Catherine Middleton.

In May, she surpassed George III, becoming the second longest-reigning monarch in the history of Britain following Victoria. During May, she also made a trip to Ireland, and became the first British monarch that visited the Irish republic as well as the first since 1911 to set foot in Ireland. She celebrated her "Diamond Jubilee" in 2012, which marked 60 years as Queen. She then passed Victoria's reign on September 9, 2015.

She is known for favoring simplicity in the court life and for taking an informed and serious role in their government, apart from the ceremonial and traditional duties.

As far as her private life is concerned, she is a keen horsewoman; she owns racehorses, attends races frequently, and occasionally visits the stud farms in Kentucky, located in the United States.

PRESIDENT REAGAN AND QUEEN ELIZABETH II HORSEBACK RIDING

She has also had a lifelong fondness of the breed of dogs called Pembroke Welsh Corgis. This fondness for corgis started with Dookie in 1933, who was the first one her family owned.

It also has been told that she has been witnessed enjoying an informal, relaxed home life occasionally with her and her family as from time to time, they will prepare a meal together and then wash up afterwards.

Her property and financial holdings make her one of the richest women throughout the world.

Now that you have learned quite a bit about Queen Elizabeth II, are you ready to go for a visit? Maybe you can catch her in the United States.

For additional information about Queen Elizabeth II, you can visit your local library, research the internet, and ask questions of your teachers, family and friends.

Visit

BABY PROFESSOR
EDUCATION KIDS

www.BabyProfessorBooks.com
to download Free Baby Professor eBooks
and view our catalog of new and exciting
Children's Books